DENES AGAY'S LEARNING TO PLAY PIANO
EASY MUSIC THEORY

INTRODUCTION

This book is intended to complement the first volume in the acclaimed series Denes Agay's Learning To Play Piano, although it can also be used as a self-contained book in its own right.

It focusses on the theory covered in Book 1 of the series, introducing various fun activities to aid understanding of the music theory concepts and introduce enjoyment to the child's overall learning process.

Inside you will find a range of intriguing games and puzzles, each associated with fundamental points covered in Learning To Play Piano, Book 1.

Easy Music Theory also includes fun stickers which c.... as incentives for children to complete each topic. The .... back of the book provides a quick reference to the ....ns.

Wise Publications
part of The Music Sales Group
London / New York / Paris / Sydney / Copenhagen / Berlin / Madrid / Hong Kong / Tokyo

Published by
Wise Publications
14-15 Berners Street, London W1T 3LJ, UK

Exclusive Distributors:
Music Sales Limited
Distribution Centre, Newmarket Road,
Bury St Edmunds, Suffolk IP33 3YB, UK
Music Sales Pty Limited
Units 3-4, 17 Willfox Street, Condell Park,
NSW 2200, Australia.

Order No. AM1004003
ISBN 978-1-78038-281-4

Puzzles devised by Christopher Hussey
Edited by Ruth Power
Illustrated by Jon Burgerman
Designed by Lizzie Barrand

Printed in the EU

www.musicsales.com

Your Guarantee of Quality
As publishers, we strive to produce every book
to the highest commercial standards.
The music has been freshly engraved and the book has
been carefully designed to minimise awkward page turns
and to make playing from it a real pleasure.
Particular care has been given to specifying acid-free,
neutral-sized paper made from pulps which have not been
elemental chlorine bleached. This pulp is from farmed
sustainable forests and was produced with special regard
for the environment.
Throughout, the printing and binding have been planned
to ensure a sturdy, attractive publication which should
give years of enjoyment.
If your copy fails to meet our high standards,
please inform us and we will gladly replace it.

THE MUSICAL ALPHABET

The theory...

LETTER NAMES OF THE WHITE KEYS

Down: Lower tones to the left   **Up:** Higher tones to the right

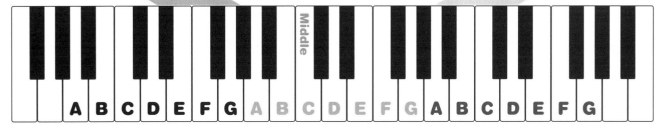

A B C D E F G A B C D E F G A B C D E F G

FINGER NAMES

Left Hand   Right Hand

5 4 3 2 1   1 2 3 4 5

- On a piano, try to find a G

- Now, try to find a higher G — then find an E below Middle C

- What is the letter name of the notes marked with a triangle below?

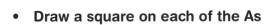

- Draw a square on each of the As

- Now, draw a circle on each of the Fs

- How many Es are there on this diagram?

...and now for the fun!

THE MUSICAL ALPHABET

Odd-one-out

Spot the note which is incorrectly named in each of the following and draw a ring around its letter name.

Then, write the correct name for each of these wrong notes into the appropriate box below to reveal the mystery musical term.

1

C D B F G A B

2

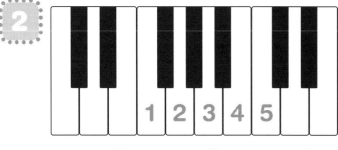

1 = F   2 = G   3 = A
4 = D   5 = C

3

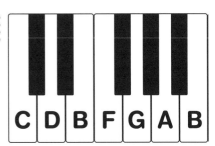

1 = C   2 = D   3 = A
4 = F   5 = G

4

F G A B G D E

5

C D E F G A B C D G

6

B G A B C D E F G A B

Mystery musical term: T R ⬚1 ⬚2 L ⬚3   ⬚4 L ⬚5 ⬚6

4

THE MUSICAL ALPHABET
Missing letters

Work out the name of each note marked with an x

and fill in the missing letters to solve the mystery words below.

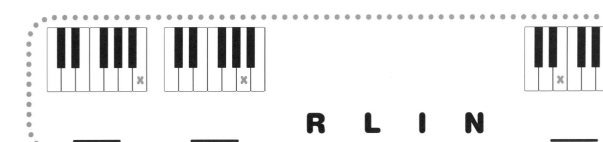

__ __ R L I N __

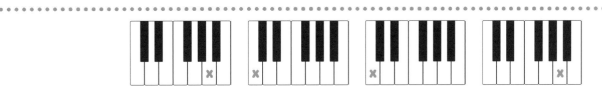

S T __ __ __ __ T O

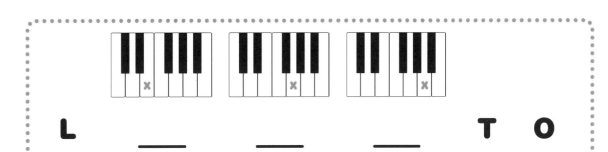

L __ __ __ T O

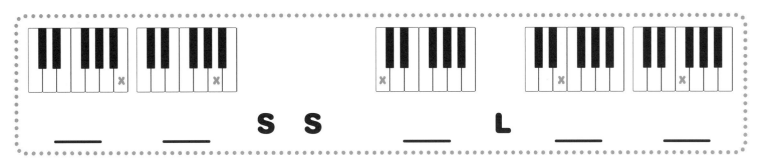

__ __ S S __ L __ __

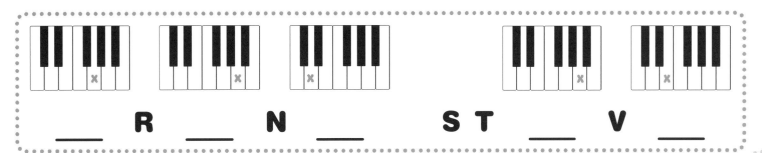

__ R __ N __ S T __ V __

THE MUSICAL ALPHABET
Wordspell

On each keyboard diagram below, the notes marked x spell out a word reading from low to high (left to right). Work out the letter names of the notes and write them in the boxes to solve the puzzle.

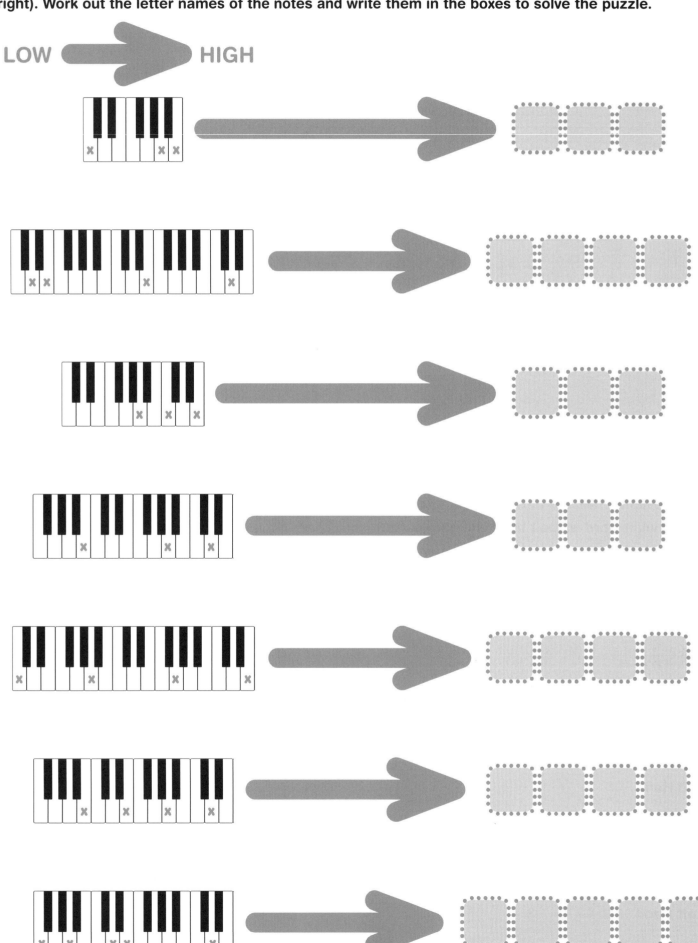

THE MUSICAL ALPHABET
Guess the tune

Find this **right hand** position on your piano:

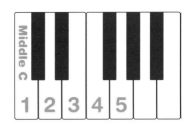

Now, play the tunes in the boxes below and see if you can guess what they are. Draw a line connecting the boxes with the correct title.

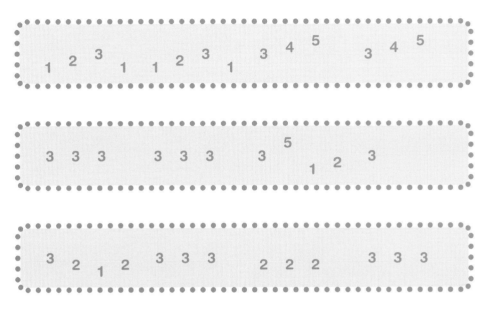

Merrily We Roll Along

Jingle Bells

Frère Jacques

Finger spelling

Using the hand positions in the keyboard diagram, work out what word is spelt by each finger pattern below, writing the letters on the lines. Then, draw a line to connect the words with their pictures.

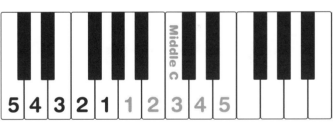

Left Hand   **Right Hand**

Right Hand   5

Left Hand   1   1

Word: __ __ __

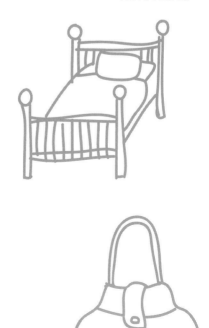

Right Hand   2
                        1

Left Hand   1

Word: __ __ __

Right Hand   2   4

Left Hand   3

Word: __ __ __

The theory...

NOTE VALUES AND RESTS

♪ = **quaver** (eighth-note) = half a count

♩ = **crotchet** (quarter-note) = one count

𝅗𝅥 = **minim** (half-note) = two counts

𝅗𝅥· = **dotted minim** (dotted half-note) = three counts

𝅝 = **semibreve** (whole-note) = four counts

Two quavers can be joined: ♫

𝄽 = crotchet rest

▬ = minim rest

▬ = semibreve rest

time signature   barline

final barline

TIME SIGNATURES

4 ← The upper number tells us how many counts there are in a bar (in this case, four).

4 ← The lower number shows what kind of note receives one count (in this case, a crotchet).

Here are some more time signatures: **2/4**   **3/4**   **6/4**

• By looking at the time signature, how many crotchet counts should there be in each bar of the music below?

• The third and fourth bar have been left blank. Can you fill the third bar with the correct number of crotchets ♩ and the fourth bar with pairs of quavers ♫ ?

• Try clapping this rhythm:

...and now for the fun!

KEEPING TIME

Matching pairs

Each item in the column on the left matches one on the right.

Can you draw a line joining each matching pair?

The first one has been done for you.

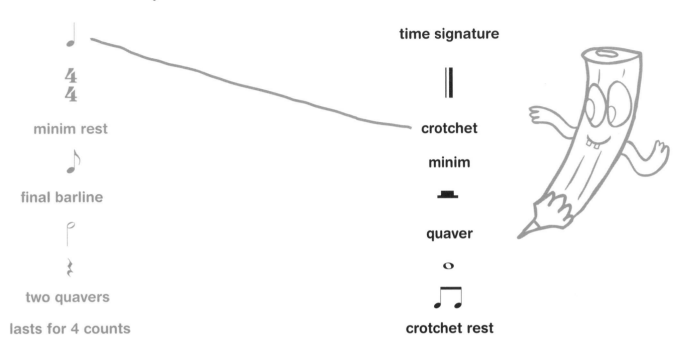

time signature

crotchet

minim rest

final barline

two quavers

lasts for 4 counts

minim

quaver

crotchet rest

Target practice

Can you match the notes with their rests? Draw a line from the tip of each arrow to the target they should aim for.

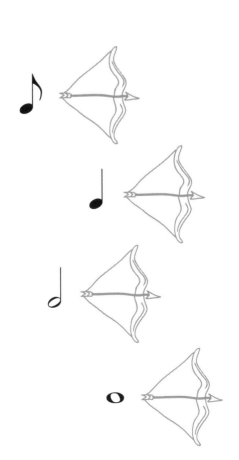

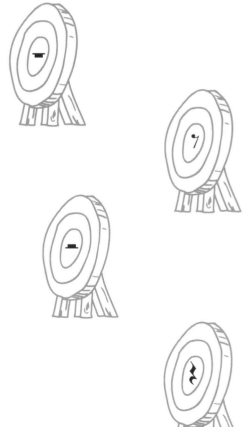

KEEPING TIME

True or false

Circle a ✓ for 'true' or a ✗ for 'false' in this quiz. Good luck!

𝄽 is a **crotchet rest**

Two **quavers** can be joined like this: ♫

♩ = a **crotchet**

▬ = a rest for two beats

3/4 tells you there are four counts in each bar

A **final barline** ‖ goes at the beginning of a piece of music

♪ = a **quaver**

♩ + ♩ = ♩.

2/4 tells you there are two counts in each bar

A ♩. lasts for two beats

𝅝 = a **semibreve**

A **time signature** goes at the start of each bar

A **semibreve** lasts for half a count

A ♩ lasts for one count

▬ is a **minim rest**

KEEPING TIME

Crossword

Solve the clues to complete this crossword.

Across

2. Which note lasts for one count? (8)

5. This note 𝅝 is called a ____________ (9)

7. 𝅗𝅥. is called a _________ minim (6)

9. What is a note that lasts two counts called? (5)

10. What do you find at the end of each bar? (7)

11. ♪ is called a _________ (6)

12. 𝄽 lasts for _____ count(s) (3)

Down

1. 𝄼 lasts for _____ count(s) (3)

3. These signs 𝄾 𝄽 𝄻 are all types of what? (5)

4. What shows you how many counts there are in each bar? (4, 9)

6. ♩ + ♫ + 𝅗𝅥 = how many counts? (4)

8. $\frac{3}{4}$ tells you there are _______ counts in each bar (5)

KEEPING TIME

Musical maths

Can you balance the seesaws below by adding the number of counts on the left together and then writing the answer on the right hand side of the seesaw?

The first one has been done for you.

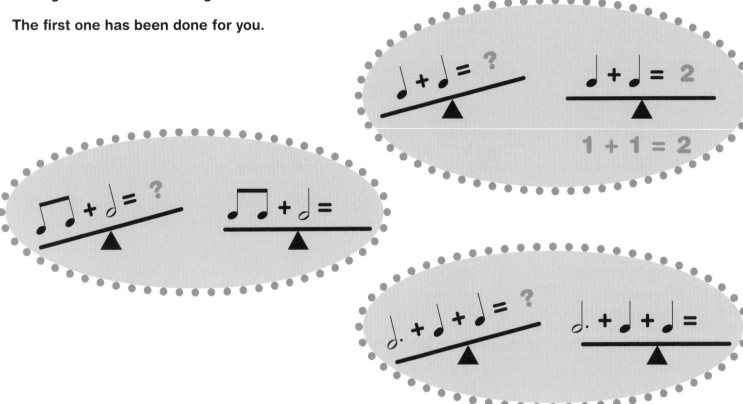

Now choose one note from the bag to balance each seesaw, drawing the note on the right hand side of the seesaw.

KEEPING TIME
Missing things!

In the music below, all the barlines are missing. Look carefully at the **time signature** to see how many counts should be in each bar, and then draw the barlines in. The first barline has been drawn in for you.

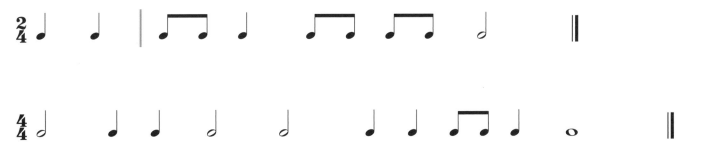

Next, fill in the missing number at the top of the time signatures in the phrases below, which should show how many crotchet beats there are in each bar.

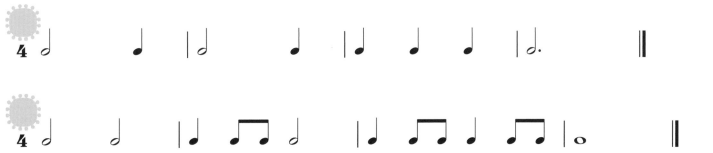

...And in the next two excerpts, there are notes missing! Write one note under each of the arrows below to make the right number of counts in each bar.

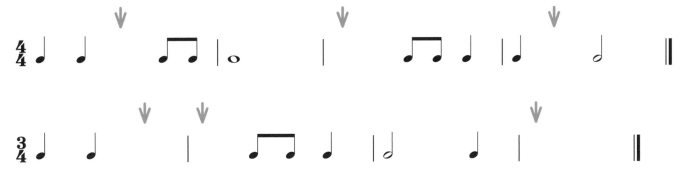

Finally, all of the stems are missing in this piece. Work out whether each note should be a quaver ♪, crotchet ♩ or minim ♩, and draw in the stems as appropriate, filling in the notehead where necessary.

Counts:

MUSICAL SIGNS
The theory...

CLEFS

 = **treble clef** (or **G clef**), which heads the treble stave, used for higher notes

𝄢 = **bass clef** (or **F clef**), which heads the bass stave, used for lower notes

CHANGING THE PITCH OF A NOTE

♯ = **sharp sign**, raising a note to the very next key (to the right)

♭ = **flat sign**, lowering a note to the very next key (to the left)

♮ = **natural sign**, which cancels a sharp or a flat sign

THE REPEAT SIGN

:‖ This sign tells you to repeat the preceding section of music.

- Trace over the clefs below and then write two more treble clefs and two more bass clefs of your own.

- Write a sharp sign before each note:

- In the music below, write a flat sign before each note except the last one — write a natural sign before this one.

- On the keyboard diagram, draw a circle around the F♯ (F sharp), E♭ (E flat) and B♭ (B flat).

...turn the page for more musical signs

MORE MUSICAL SIGNS

The theory...

LOUDS AND SOFTS

p = **piano** = soft mp = **mezzo piano** = medium soft

f = **forte** = loud mf = **mezzo forte** = medium loud

———————— = **crescendo** (or **cresc.**) = gradually louder

———————— = **diminuendo** (or **dim.**) = gradually softer

OTHER SIGNS

= **staccato** = play this note short and detached

= **slur** = a curved line joining different notes, telling you to play **legato** (smoothly)

= **accent** = stress this note

rit. = **ritardando** = gradually slower

- Add a **staccato** dot, above or below the notehead, to each note in bar 1 and 2 that doesn't already have one.

- Now, add a **slur** to each pair of quavers in bar 3 that doesn't have one.

- Add an **accent**, above or below the notehead, to each note in bar 4 that doesn't already have one.

- Now, add the sign for 'loud' under the music at the beginning of bar 2.

- Add the sign for 'soft' under the music at the beginning of bar 3.

- Try playing this tune on a piano.

...and now for the fun!

MUSICAL SIGNS
Wordsearch

The names of lots of musical signs are listed at the bottom of this page. They are hidden in the grid, where they are written horizontally, vertically and diagonally, forwards and backwards.

See if you can find them and put a ring around them.

E	F	E	L	C	S	S	A	B	J	S	H	A
R	T	O	D	N	A	T	U	R	A	L	T	O
I	I	R	T	I	M	A	E	L	L	E	G	C
T	R	E	B	L	E	C	L	E	F	C	R	L
A	R	P	A	E	Z	C	F	G	R	E	H	S
R	C	T	M	Z	Z	A	O	A	S	T	L	H
D	W	C	E	E	O	T	R	T	P	U	S	A
A	I	M	E	Z	Z	O	F	O	R	T	E	R
N	O	M	D	N	S	Z	D	B	A	S	A	I
D	A	T	I	R	T	N	O	L	H	L	O	N
O	C	A	T	N	E	S	F	P	S	Y	E	U
X	C	R	E	C	U	H	B	T	I	R	D	E
S	E	H	S	X	G	E	A	A	I	A	P	N
T	A	E	P	E	R	C	N	M	R	I	N	D
A	R	S	L	T	C	M	I	D	A	P	Q	O
C	T	R	E	P	A	D	C	N	O	T	E	R

treble clef	bass clef	repeat
sharp	flat	natural
mezzo piano	mezzo forte	slur
staccato	legato	accent
ritardando	crescendo	diminuendo

MUSICAL SIGNS
Codebreaker

To solve this puzzle, complete Stage 1 and then Stage 2
to reveal the mystery word.

Stage 1

In this stack of balls, how many of each of the following are there?

?

✳ **treble clefs:** ✳

➕ soft (**piano**) signs: ➕

⬤ medium soft (**mezzo piano**) signs: ◯

▣ **staccato** notes: ▣

★ **slurs:** ★

◆ **sharp** signs: ◆

✖ loud (**forte**) signs: ✖

◈ **bass clefs:** ◈

◎ quavers with **accents:** ◎

▣ **flat** signs: ▣

Stage 2

Now, write each answer into the correct circle below, then use the key to break the code and work out
the mystery word.

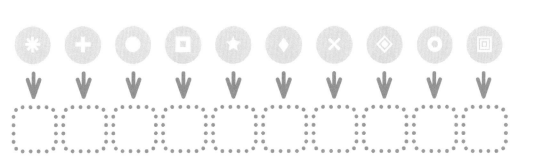

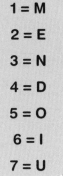

KEY:

1 = M

2 = E

3 = N

4 = D

5 = O

6 = I

7 = U

MUSICAL SIGNS
Matching pairs

Match each musical sign in the box with its name or meaning
and draw a curvy line (avoiding any collisions!) connecting them.
The first one has been drawn for you.

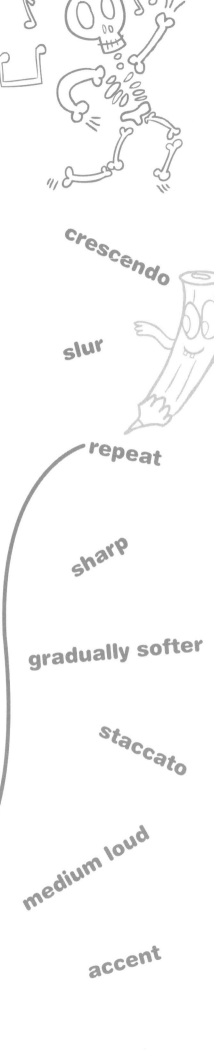

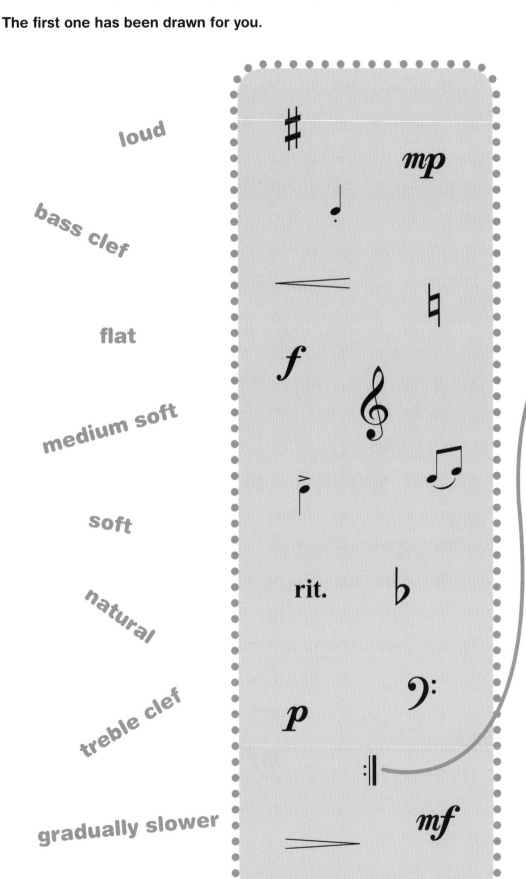

loud

bass clef

flat

medium soft

soft

natural

treble clef

crescendo

slur

repeat

sharp

gradually softer

staccato

medium loud

accent

18

MUSICAL SIGNS

Odd-one-out

In each of the clouds below, there is an odd-one-out that doesn't belong with the rest of the group. Work out which one it is in each case and draw a ring around it.

Now, draw each odd-one-out into the cloud they should be in.

MUSICAL SIGNS

Keyword

Identify each musical sign below and write its name in the row of blank boxes next to it. The first letter of each missing word has been given to you.

The column of boxes with circles spells out a mystery word. Solve this 'keyword' as soon as you can as it will reveal some more missing letters.

Keyword

?

♮ = N ☐ ☐ ☐ Ⓡ ☐

p = P ◯ ☐ ☐ ☐

This clef 𝄞 is called a _____ clef: Ⓣ ☐ ☐ ☐ ☐ ☐ ☐

♩ = S ☐ ◯ ☐ ☐ ☐

♪♪ = S ☐ ☐ ◯

> = D ☐ ☐ ☐ ☐ ◯ ☐ ☐

♯ = S ☐ ◯ ☐ ☐

♪ = A ☐ ☐ ◯ ☐

< = C ☐ ☐ ☐ ☐ ◯ ☐ ☐

f = F ◯ ☐ ☐ ☐

Keyword: Ⓡ ◯ Ⓣ ◯ ◯ ◯ ◯ ◯ ◯ ◯

Keyword clue: This musical term tells you to get 'gradually slower'.

ON THE STAVE
The theory...

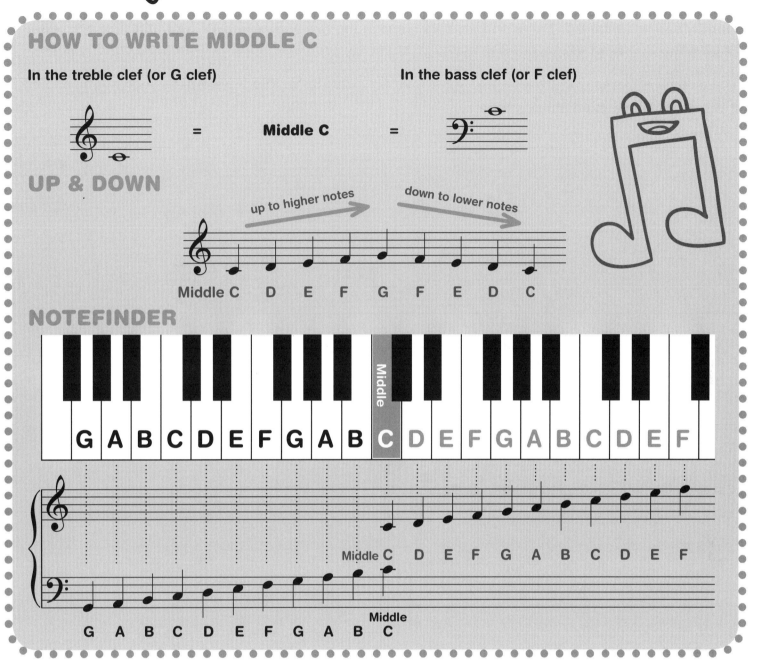

HOW TO WRITE MIDDLE C

In the treble clef (or G clef)   In the bass clef (or F clef)

= **Middle C** =

UP & DOWN

up to higher notes   down to lower notes

Middle C   D   E   F   G   F   E   D   C

NOTEFINDER

G A B C D E F G A B **Middle C** C D E F G A B C D E F

Middle C   D   E   F   G   A   B   C   D   E   F

G A B C D E F G A B **Middle C**

• Write the names of the notes in the treble clef in the boxes below.

notes in spaces   **notes on lines**

up   up

[F] [ ] [ ] [ ]   [E] [ ] [ ] [ ] [ ]

• In the music below, put a flat sign ♭ before each note B and a sharp sign ♯ before each note F.

crotchet   minim

• Two notes are missing above. Put a crotchet on the note A in bar 3 and a minim on the note G in bar 4.

21

ON THE STAVE

Which clef?

Write either a treble clef 🎼 or a bass clef 𝄢 at the start of each of the following, so that the letter names are correct.

The first one has been done for you.

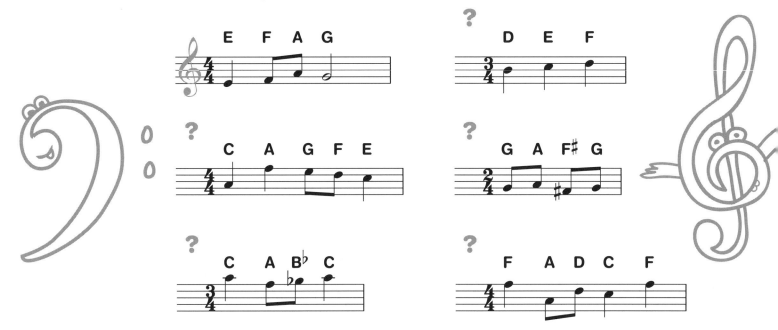

Which letter name?

For each of the following notes, ring its correct name below. The first one has been done for you.

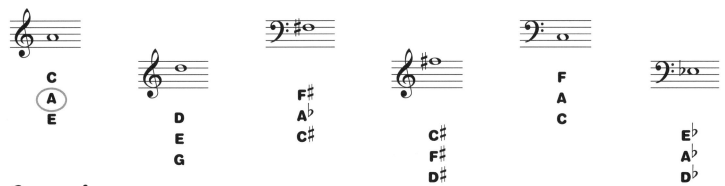

Count up

Look at the tune below, then answer the questions.

In this music...

- How many Fs are there?
- How many crotchets are there?
- How many B♭s are there?

ON THE STAVE

Wordspell

Each series of notes in the boxes below spells out a mystery word. To solve this puzzle, write the letter name of each note on the line beneath it to reveal the mystery words.

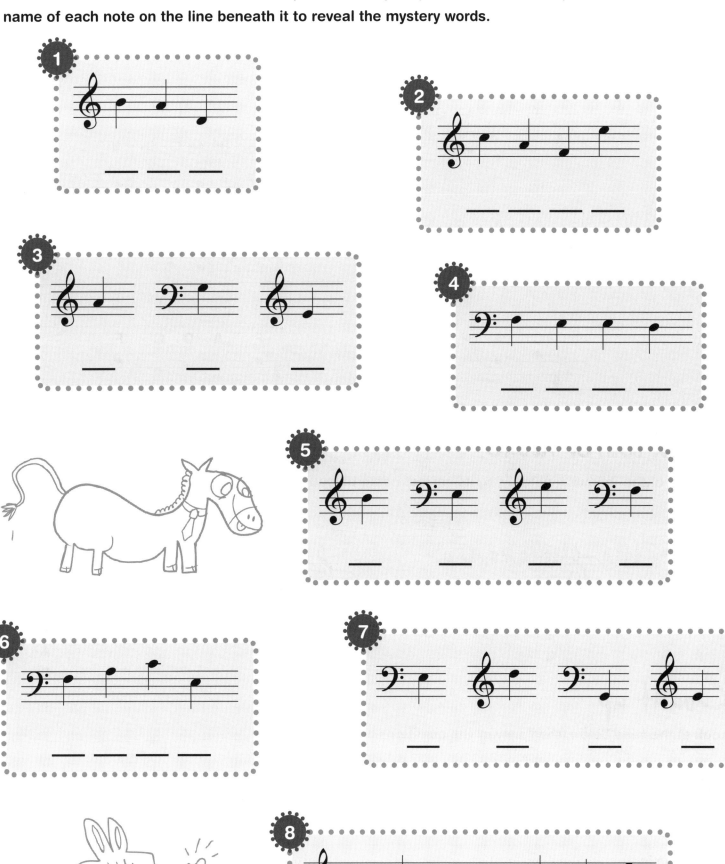

ON THE STAVE

Wrong notes!

In each of the examples below, cross out the wrong letter names
and write the correct name of the note above.
The first one has been done for you.

Spot-the-difference

There are eight differences between tune **A** and tune **B**. Can you find them and circle them on tune **B**?

24

NOTE-TO-NOTE

The theory...

STEPS, SKIPS AND REPETITIONS

Notes on the stave may move by:

Steps from line to next space, or from space to next line.

Skips with one line or one space between the two notes.

Repetition stays on the same line or in the same space.

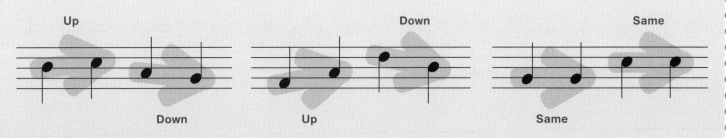

Up

Down

Down

Up

Same

Same

INTERVALS

The distance between two notes is called an **interval**. An interval is measured and named according to the number of notes involved.

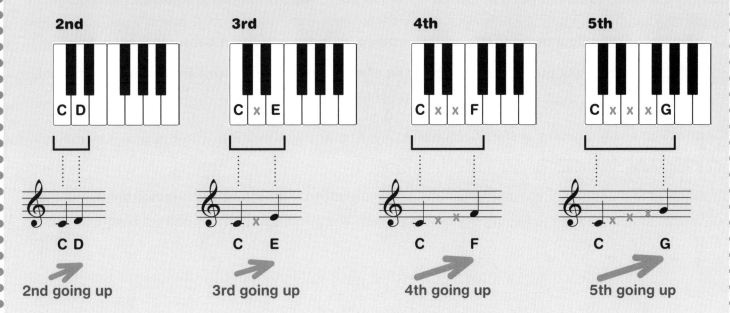

2nd

C D

C D

2nd going up

3rd

C x E

C E

3rd going up

4th

C x x F

C F

4th going up

5th

C x x x G

C G

5th going up

MELODIC INTERVALS

2nd   3rd   4th   5th

HARMONIC INTERVALS

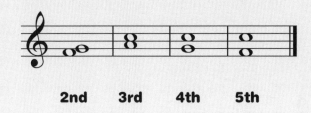

2nd   3rd   4th   5th

...and now for the fun!

NOTE-TO-NOTE

Skips and steps

Ring all the **skips**, up or down, in the excerpts below. The first has been done for you.

Now, in the same excerpts, put a box around pairs of notes that have a **step** between them (up or down), like this:

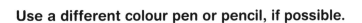

Use a different colour pen or pencil, if possible.

Interval puzzle

For each of the notes in a square, follow the arrow and move the note by the **interval** written in the rectangle. Then, draw a line joining the rectangle with the circle that has the correct new note in it.

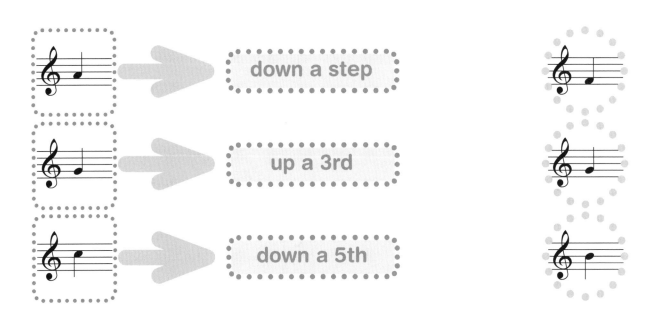

NOTE-TO-NOTE

Odd-one-out

On the flags below, there are a mixture of **melodic** and **harmonic intervals**. Can you spot the odd-one-out in each bag and draw a ring around it?

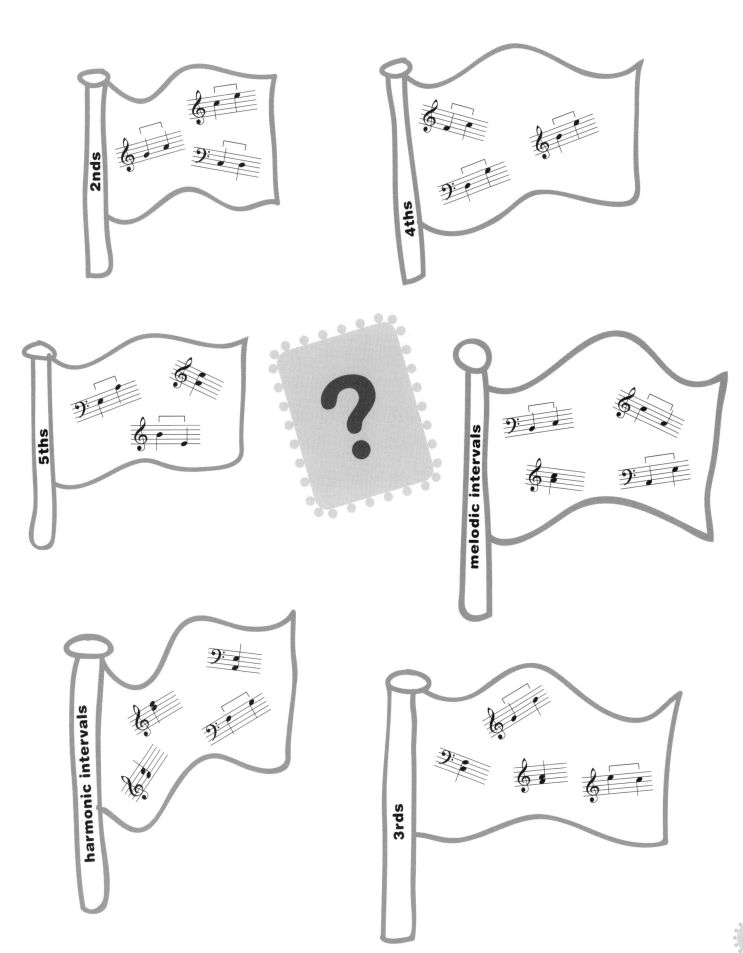

NOTE-TO-NOTE
Mystery word

Starting with the written note, move the note by the **interval** shown by the arrows that follow, writing the new note in the next box after each move. Write its letter name on the line underneath. Work through the sequence, copying the last note's letter name into the square in the mystery word column.

Do this for each line of music to complete the puzzle and solve the mystery word.

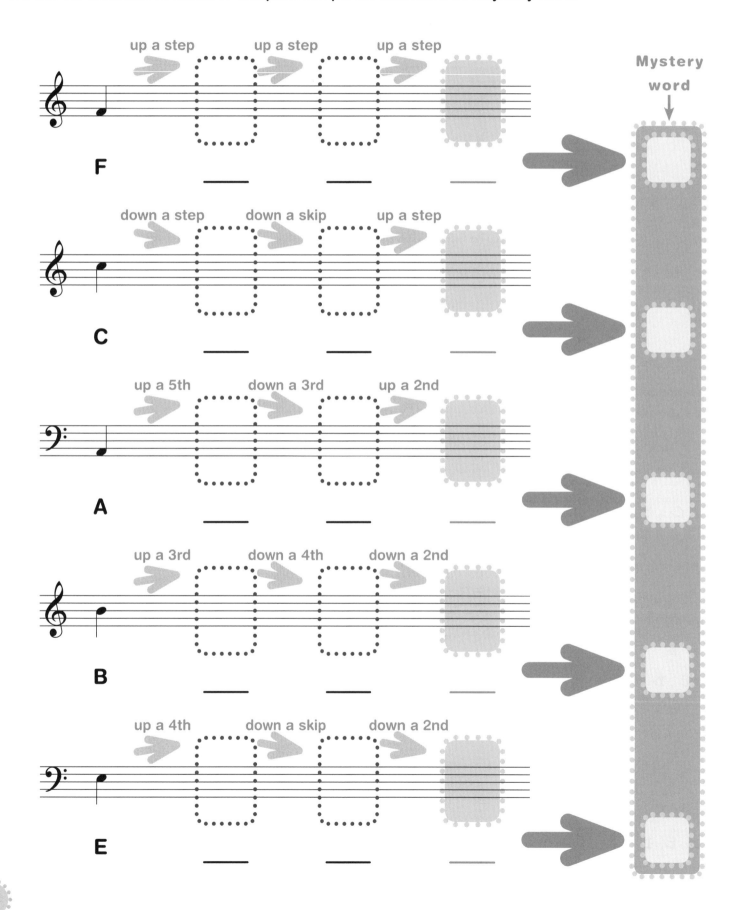

ANSWERS:

PAGE 4 Odd-one-out

1 C D **B** F G A B

2
1 2 3 **4** 5
1 = F   2 = G   3 = A
4 = **D**   5 = C

3
1 2 **3** 4 5
1 = C   2 = D   3 = **A**
4 = F   5 = G

4 F G A B **G** D E

5 C D E F G A B C D **G**

6 **B** G A B C D E F G A B

Mystery musical term: **T R E B L E   C L E F**

PAGE 7 Guess the tune

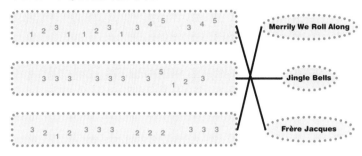

1 2   1 2   3   3 4 5   3 4 5 — **Merrily We Roll Along**

3 3 3   3 3 3   3   5 1 2 3 — **Jingle Bells**

3 2 1   3 3 3   2 2 2   3 3 3 — **Frère Jacques**

Finger spelling

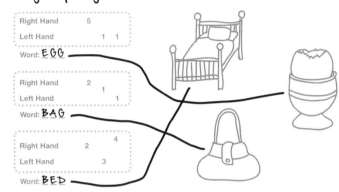

| Right Hand | 5 |
| Left Hand | 1 1 |
| Word: E G G |

| Right Hand | 2 1 |
| Left Hand | 1 |
| Word: B A G |

| Right Hand | 2 4 |
| Left Hand | 3 |
| Word: B E D |

GE 5 Missing letters

B**AR**LINE

STACCATO

LEGATO

BASS CLEF

GRAND STAVE

GE 6 Wordspell

C A B

D E E D

A C E

B A D

C A G E

B E A D

FADED

PAGE 9 Matching pairs

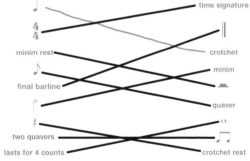

time signature — crotchet — minim — quaver — crotchet rest
4/4 — minim rest — final barline — two quavers — lasts for 4 counts

Target practice

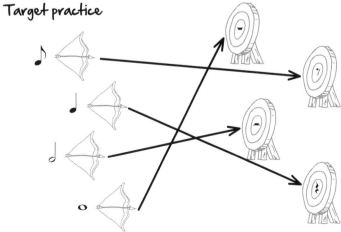

PAGE 10 True or False

1. ✓
2. ✓
3. ✗
4. ✓
5. ✗
6. ✗
7. ✓
8. ✓
9. ✓
10. ✗
11. ✓
12. ✗
13. ✗
14. ✓
15. ✗

29

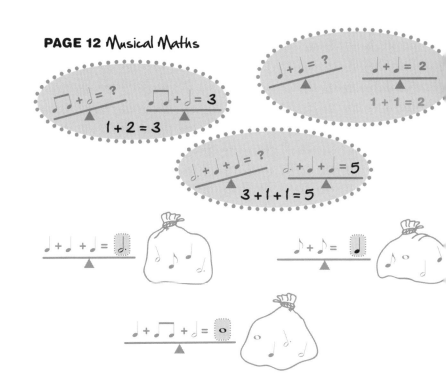

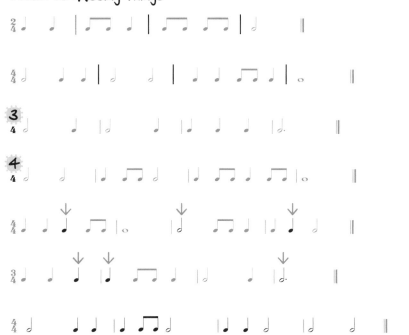

E	F	E	L	C	S	S	A	B	J	S	H	A
R	T	O	D	N	A	T	U	R	A	L	T	O
I	I	R	T	I	M	A	E	L	L	E	G	C
T	R	E	B	L	E	C	L	E	F	C	R	L
A	R	P	A	E	Z	C	F	G	R	E	H	S
R	C	T	M	Z	Z	A	O	A	S	T	L	H
D	W	C	E	E	O	T	R	T	P	U	S	A
A	I	M	E	Z	Z	O	F	O	R	T	E	R
N	O	M	D	N	S	Z	D	B	A	S	A	I
D	A	T	I	R	T	N	O	L	H	L	O	N
O	C	A	T	N	E	S	F	P	S	Y	E	U
X	C	R	E	C	U	H	B	T	I	R	D	E
S	E	H	S	X	G	E	A	A	I	A	P	N
T	A	E	P	E	R	C	N	M	R	I	N	D
A	R	S	L	T	C	M	I	D	A	P	Q	O
C	T	R	E	P	A	D	C	N	O	T	E	R

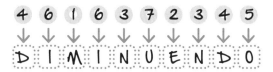

4 6 1 6 3 7 2 3 4 5
↓ ↓ ↓ ↓ ↓ ↓ ↓ ↓ ↓ ↓
D I M I N U E N D O

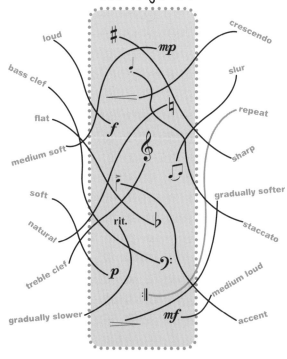

Odd-one-out

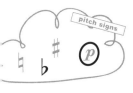
pitch signs

notes with slurs

signs that change tempo (speed)

notes with accents

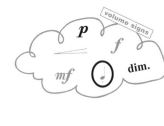
clefs

volume signs

staccato notes

PAGE 20 Keyword

Keyword

♮ = N A T U R A L

𝑝 = P I A N O

This clef 𝄞 is called a _____ clef: T R E B L E

♪ = S T A C C A T O

♪ = S L U R

⟍ = D I M I N U E N D O

♯ = S H A R P

♪ = A C C E N T

⟋ = C R E S C E N D O

𝑓 = F O R T E

Keyword: R I T A R D A N D O

AGE 22 Which clef?

E F A G

D E F

C A G F E

G A F♯ G

C A B♭ C

F A D C F

which letter name?

C A E

D E G

F♯ A♭ C♯

F♯ D♯

F A C

E♭ A♭ D♭

count up

How many Fs are there? **6**

How many crotchets are there? **4**

How many B♭s are there? **2**

AGE 23 Wordspell

1. B A D
2. C A F E
3. A G E
4. F E E D
5. B E E F
6. F A C E
7. E D G E
8. C A B B A G E

PAGE 24 Wrong notes!

G E A E D G (F, C)

B♭ F
A A A G A A C

F A
E A G E F A

B♭ G
D G F G♯ G A C D

E G A
F♯ G A B D♯ F♯ E

Spot-the-difference

B

PAGE 26 Skips and steps

Interval puzzle

down a step

up a 3rd

down a 5th

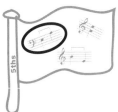
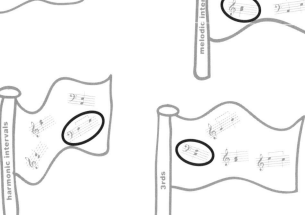

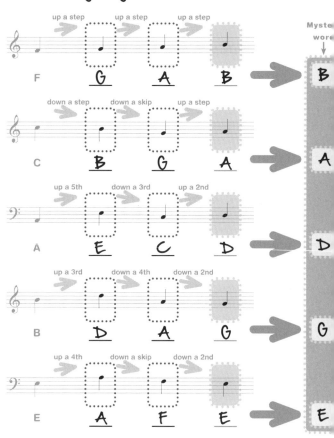

Also available in the series...

DENES AGAY'S LEARNING TO PLAY PIANO
EASY BOOGIE & BLUES

A fun collection of 18 tunes
perfect for beginners to explore
the exciting musical styles of
jazz, boogie and blues

AM1003970

DENES AGAY'S LEARNING TO PLAY PIANO
EASY CLASSICAL THEMES

A fun collection of 18 popular pieces
perfect for inspiring beginners
to explore the classical
music style

AM1003981

DENES AGAY'S LEARNING TO PLAY PIANO
EASY PIANO SCALES

Perfect for inspiring young pianists!
Making learning and playing scales fun

AM100

Easy Boogie & Blues, **Easy** Classical Themes and **Easy** Piano Scales each contain a repertoire specially devised to complement Denes Agay's piano tutor series.

The pieces in these books have been carefully chosen and sequenced to reflect the incremental skills covered throughout the complete four-book tutor series.

Through these themed compilations children are introduced to a rewarding selection of music that will inspire them to get the most out of this famous learning method.